CW00840095

Free Your Mind: Change Your Life!

By

Karen Frances Maya Bromley

'We all deserve to live a happy, fulfilled abundant life; there is enough abundance for everyone'!

With Love and Peace Karen x

Dedicated to my beautiful niece Emma; you are just like the daughter I always wished for, a gift to us all.

May your life's journey be brimming with abundance, happiness love and magic......

I love you to the moon and back. K.K

xxxxxxxxx

Contents

Chapters

Acknowledgments - *huge thanks to all these fabulous people:*

Sue for her strength and ongoing love and support.

My wonderful dad for giving me a home and space to heal.

My beautiful mum and Bern for always being there for me.

My amazing, strong, fabulous friends! Especially Hilary Lees, www.essence-coaching.com work / career transition coach. Jacqueline for lending me her beautiful home to   write.

Bailey my rehomed dog aka Angel for her love and loyalty!

My ex - husband for being the greatest teacher in my life.

Kim Bromley, Hypnotherapist and Wellness Coach.

Denise Sturch my wonderful psychic friend who helped give me the strength to start my new life and for her continued guided support.

My inspiring tutors Sue, Shola and Susan Osborne (amazing woman!).

For my amazing business connections in Norfolk:

Karin Carruthers design communication at www.screambluemurder.co.uk

'Ola' Femi Olasehinde; for my website videos www.jammo.org.uk

Web designer; Brian at www.castonwebdesigns.co.uk

Lisa North photography and Sapphira Marples; video editing.

Leon Zaal; business coach www.actioncoach.com.

Eleanor Lewis; financial advisor St James' Place wealth management.

I am blessed to be part of the online

'Transformation TV' hidden teachers of the world!

Testimonials

'In my sessions, I was able to pinpoint a block given to me when I was young, that I wasn't clever enough or good enough to achieve my high ambitions. I felt this mental block losing its energy and I am now confident in building my business without the previous 'mental' constraints; amazing techniques!' K.C

'Karen, what you have done for me is incredible. For the first time, I feel in control and I look and feel different. You've changed my life! A.R

'I cannot thank you enough for helping me to see how my life was unfolding and that I needed to take control. You are wonderful!' D.S

'This has been a really interesting experience and I have learnt a lot about myself. Thanks!' L.W

'I have felt so much better about myself and have had lots more energy. Thank you'! L.H

'This process turned out to be more interesting, surprising and revealing than I anticipated. It helped me to summon up my own ideas and plans and to explore them. It makes you think, reflect, consider and plan!' I.P

'Karen has so much empathy for her clients and intuitively knows what to do so emotional barriers to recovery can be overturned. The support Karen gave me at a really difficult time was invaluable. She played a huge part in helping me achieve the right mind set to move forwards with my life in the best possible way.' C.S

Chapter 1: Why read my book

You no longer need to keep living your life with restrictions. I am here to introduce you to 'The Maya Method' so you can free your mind and change your life!

Why wait?

I wasted too many years being 'stuck' in negative belief systems and negative thinking and you do not have to.

You will see when you read the story of how I transformed my life that I used the power of my mind and it blew my mind totally!

I talk about my experiences of having M.E for years but this book is for everyone, whatever you have been through; it is all about moving from being 'stuck' to living your abundant life.

I was so inspired during my transformation that I trained to be a Hypnotherapist and Wellness

Coach (I was already doing Reiki Healing), and I feel very passionate about supporting you to transform your life.

The people I support are all in the same situation: feeling 'stuck' in their life for one reason or another. It does not matter what the reason is, it's a symptom leading to what is really going on. Deep inside, the subconscious mind is driving their lives - just as it was for me.

Our beliefs are a result of past programming from others around us when we were children. We live believing we cannot change what we have internalised; that we are what we are. The truth is we can change our beliefs!

With guidance you can change the beliefs that drive your thoughts, actions and behaviours through the power of your amazing subconscious mind.

It is like wearing negative glasses and viewing the world through these beliefs. For example, if you believe that 'I am not good enough' then your mind ignores compliments or situations that project 'I am good enough' as it doesn't match the belief stored in your subconscious mind. Therefore, you can miss out on positive opportunities and relationships.

It is very important for me to share this life changing knowledge and the techniques I use with you, so that you can live the abundant life you want and deserve!

By reading this book you will understand that there's a wonderful positive way forward as I explain what I learnt in the transformation of my life. I'll introduce you to what I have created and called: 'The Maya Method', with the steps and tools to transform your life.

I use coaching, counselling skills, inner child therapy and NLP (neuro linguistic programming) techniques and hypnotherapy with 'The Maya Method' to make these lasting powerful changes in your subconscious mind.

You can feel confident, fulfilled and happy. You can believe in yourself so you have clarity and control in your life!

What do you want from your life?

You do deserve it!

I have had the pleasure of supporting clients in changing their self - limiting beliefs. Not only have they transformed their lives by being confident, fulfilled and reaching their goals but also other positive things have happened. Some have improved their sleep, others have lost weight and many have started to attract wonderful new situations and people into their lives!

Once you step into the flow of your life: you're on the path you're meant to be on, being the person you are meant to be and it all happens for you!

A wonderful abundant life awaits you!

Here is an example of a client I supported through 'The Maya Method':

A lady came to see me with low self-esteem wanting to feel self-belief. She was working in a job that she did not really like but she put up with it. She was not very confident and was generally unhappy even though she thought she should not be as she had a good life generally.

Once she realised the negative self-beliefs she'd picked up in childhood and changed them to really positive beliefs, she accepted who she was, her identity and her role in life started to become clear. She left her job as she now felt worthy as they were not treating her with respect. She applied for jobs that she would love to do and even negotiated a higher salary in the job she wanted!

Her mood lifted and her doctor started to take her off her anti-depressant medication.

Her self-belief soared. Her husband and the people around her noted that she was the most positive they had ever seen her! She found her direction in life and connected with who she truly was. She noticed she now had an opinion, felt free and had lots of energy. She was enjoying living a healthier lifestyle including: healthy eating, maintaining a positive focus on her health and her body, plus her self-esteem went up from 30% to 100%!

When you change that core self-limiting belief it has a wonderful positive knock on effect on your whole life! This then affects others around you too!

Chapter 2: My Story

I was on my hands and knees in the spare room, with my head on the floor as I prayed for my life to end............. I prayed with such desperation to whatever is out there, wanting the suffering I was experiencing to stop; I did not want to kill myself I just wanted my life to end as the symptoms of the M.E (chronic fatigue syndrome) were totally overwhelming and insufferable. I was completely stuck, lost, so desperately lonely and full of fear about everything.

The symptoms were unbearable at times: the constant aching in my muscles, the feeling of continually being stabbed in the muscles of my neck and shoulders were horrendous. The heavy restless feeling in my body and the constant feeling of overwhelming fatigue where climbing the stairs felt like I was climbing a mountain were all too much.

I wondered if I had a brain tumour as I had an awful brain fog where I could not think straight. I forgot the name of items and people that were well known to me, I had spatial awareness issues and kept bumping into the doorways.

The weirdest symptom of all was the unusual burning feeling in my head, like my brain was on fire - strange I know but sadly very true. The most difficult thing of all was that I looked normal the majority of the time so others struggled to understand what I was going through. I often wondered if people thought I was exaggerating or lying because of how they reacted to me.

The only time I looked really awful was when I had the occasional 'white out' where I did go a deathly white shade very quickly. Looking OK made it all the worse, especially with my ex-husband; it was hard enough for him to understand what I was experiencing at the best of times, but me looking outwardly OK just made it harder.

I also had a huge sensitivity to noise and lights with crippling migraines at times so the best place to be was in my bed: hiding away from life, retreating into myself, into my shell more and more.

I was feeling so sad, so lost, so stuck with negative thoughts spinning around in my head: 'why me, what have I done to deserve this, how can I live the rest of my life like this I am only 47' - over and over again, driving myself mad with my negative thoughts.

Here is a bit more information about ME. Feel free to skip this bit if need be and go to the rest of my story!

M.E. - Myalgic Encephalomyelitis

My=muscle

Algic=pain

Mye=spinal cord

Itis=inflammation

It is a neurological disease, an injury to the central nervous system. Some researchers put it down to a virus or infectious disease triggering it and overstimulating the immune system. It affects the immune system, neurological system, musculoskeletal system, endocrine and cardiovascular systems.

(www.thegracecharityforme.org/what.asp 30/06/16).

I believe that M.E is caused by a combination of stress, whether it is chemical, emotional or physical. My mind and body were under constant long periods of stress as a social worker. I first experienced problems in my gut with Irritable Bowel Syndrome and food intolerances. Then I had a flu like virus and it continued for 11 years with varying degrees of the M.E symptoms dominating my life.

The other huge stress in my life was that I was very unhappy in my marriage, I felt this quite early on but I wanted children and I was 38 so my body clock was ticking loudly by then.

Something has to give when the body is under so much stress for prolonged periods of time. Stress causes the majority of diseases and it can affect us in all sorts of ways.

The body goes into fight or flight mode and I was stuck in this high alert state for years so no wonder I 'burnt out' as I called it - starting with my gut. Doctors just kept telling me to come back in a few months if I had not improved and then eventually they diagnosed me with M.E.

I wish that my G.P had asked me what was going on in my life, asking what job I did and whether it was stressful and whether I was happy. Another important question is surely asking what I eat and drink etc. I hope that one day our health care providers will show an interest and treat us as a whole person knowing that one thing affects another and offer preventative advice and care using complementary therapies instead of just drugs!

I was one of the lucky ones, some people spend years in bed constantly or in a wheelchair. For me, in between the worst flare ups I could work part time, but when I worked I could not do much else. It was a choice between working, housework, shopping, being a wife, going out etc. I could not do more than one thing a lot of the time.

At my best I felt like I had continual flu and it was bad enough trying to pull myself together all the time and pretend I was ok to do things I needed to do to live. That was really draining in itself and of course I was just making myself worse by working in a stressful job - working with sick and needy people. I should have left social work despite the views of my ex -husband. It was my choice ultimately but I had given my power to him by then.

The flare ups of the M.E were unbearable. When I was back in bed, I felt like a victim of life, a victim of the illness and felt totally powerless. Feeling a victim left me feeling even more empty causing more 'poor me' thoughts. I was feeling so low with dark feelings churning, living and growing inside me like a monster I was feeding.

How could I keep going, how could I keep living like this? These negative thoughts took me deep down into a funnel of despair and torment - black consuming the few spaces I had left inside of me. How much darker, how much deeper could I take myself. How much lonelier could I feel?

All this time I refused hefty pain killers and anti-depressants when my doctor offered them to me, which I am very proud of looking back. The one bit of strength I had was my determination to survive this naturally. Survive was the word, that was all I thought I could do; try to survive.

I had lost my belief in myself, in my future, in my health. Early on in my marriage I had 2 miscarriages and I had lost the hope of becoming a mother. We went for adoption but I worried about my health and after getting one and a half years into the adoption process it was scuppered by the M.E.

I would not have been able to cope with adopting a child with extra needs so it was for the best. Also

I was so unhappy in my marriage it would not have been fair to expose an adopted child to the situation and we couldn't have coped as a couple.

It all seemed like it was meant to be. At the time I couldn't have left my husband to start a new life with an adopted child. It's not fair to keep subjecting a child who's already had huge life changes after being in the foster care system, to deal with even more change.

All that aside, it did not stop my yearning to be a mother. The loss of not being allowed to be in the special club of motherhood was devastating to me. My friends were all mothers and I felt an outsider. I felt so sad but I did not show it or tell them. I was always thinking of other people's feelings and trying to make it comfortable for them.

I felt a genuine thrill when my friends were pregnant but the deep dark reality inside me was of emptiness. What do you do with those feelings? My ex-husband could not cope with my feelings so I did what I had learnt to do since childhood; I pushed my feelings deep down inside myself. Where were all my feelings going and what were they doing to my health? I believe they were festering inside me.

What I was focusing on was: illness, loss, poor me, pain, grief, deep sadness and wanting to die. What a combination! Reading these words back shakes me to the core; remembering where I was and where I am now - thankfully!

I had spent a lot of time, energy and money on many complimentary therapies during those 11 years: acupuncture, counselling, nutritionist, naturopath, reiki healing, homeopath, cognitive behavioural therapy, massage therapists, chiropractor, Perrin technique with a great osteopath, biodynamic therapy, zero balancing, chakra healing etc.

Lots of these therapies did help me, but they were not moving me forward. I felt good afterwards maybe for a day or two but then my body went back to its default setting of the M.E, and I kept wondering:

'What is the secret to changing my life on all levels?'

All this time I was pretending that I was better than I was. My husband didn't want to hear how I was feeling as there was 'always something wrong with me'. Well there would be with those symptoms!

So, I became good at acting; I did not feel worthy of even telling my friends how I truly felt. Some friends just left me to it which was incredibly sad. I needed their support and the odd message or a short visit would have been so wonderful. I realise now that I was pretending to be ok when I wasn't. I don't blame them for not helping me because they didn't know.

Thank goodness I did tell Sue - the most wonderful friend you could ever want. She was my rock and still is. I let her into my real world but I still didn't tell her or show her how dark and petrifying it really was.

At that point, I had not made the connection to where I had learnt to be like this; I had not made that discovery yet.

The doctors kept saying that there was nothing they could do and I believed them - as you do don't you! Until the January day when I prayed, I prayed so hard to end my life and my life did end but luckily not literally but ended as I knew it!

Guidance and synchronicities came to me in the form of a hypnotherapist and wellness coach who started working in the next village where I had reiki healing. Her name is Kim Bromley and of course I am Karen Bromley so the universe very kindly sent me another Bromley to support me to transform my life and she was really great! This is where my journey of transformation started!

Kim listened as I sobbed my heart out. She psychologically held up a mirror to show me my life and I realised that I had slipped deep, deep down into the role of a victim. I was shocked and surprised which confused me a lot at first but it all started to make sense!

The first major surprise was how I was avoiding my feelings about living in my deeply unhappy marriage. With Kim's gentle help I realised that I had to face this. I now knew that all along I had avoided acknowledging my unhappy marriage because facing it meant finally doing something about it.

This was very difficult as my ex - husband did not want to talk to me on an emotional level generally, let alone about my feelings and flagging up our marriage as a huge problem to me, so I planned what I was going to say with Kim's help which gave me the strength.

He was not interested and threw it back in my face and he definitely didn't want marriage counselling. I wondered how I ended up in this mess. The warning signs about my husband were there before we married. He didn't accept who I had been before we met when I was in my partying years during my mid to late twenties. He had a real issue with how I had previously lived my life which I always found strange since I met him at the age of 38. By this point I had well and truly outgrown my explorative years!

Initially, we argued a lot, especially after drinking alcohol as I stood my ground. Then I started to give in to keep the peace and allowed comments to chip away at my confidence and self-esteem.

Now I realise that I gave my personal power to him and I started to lose the essence of who I was. He was generally a good man, a popular, kind, fun man but he had issues and I now realise that this was his problem and not mine and that it seemed an unconscious pattern of his to do this.

Anyway, at the time I was changing, I could have gone back into my lonely shell but I was starting to grow as a person so I bravely kept taking a step forward as it were. I knew I had hit rock bottom emotionally which in a sense was the best place to be as the only way was up!

I drew a line under my past and took responsibility for my life, my health, my thoughts, beliefs and actions which was hugely important as I had given my power away.

So I started to reconnect with my power and this was fuelling me to do more, to change more, and to go for it! I started to believe in me; I tentatively started to let go of all those stored emotions and beliefs; the more I let go of them and the more I faced my fears, the more I moved forward.

I realised that I had also given my personal power to my social work career too and that I was trying to save the world! I had given my power to everyone else in my care. Giving time and energy to myself and my needs was my lowest priority because I didn't feel worthy.

Trying to be everything to everybody became common place. I wondered why I did that! This started me thinking; it was amazing to step back and to finally see what I had been doing and I wanted to know why I had done these things.

This started my quest to understand myself and to heal myself as I believed that I could transform my life if I kept asking, reading, learning and changing. Thank goodness it worked!

What I discovered will unfold as I share my story with you further and introduce you to 'The Maya Method', created from my experiences.

So, I used techniques to take my personal power back and to boost my power, which was liberating! I read some personal growth books and listened to great free personal growth webinars which really inspired me and helped to keep my positive thinking and beliefs going.

I struggled to read for a long time in the beginning but I started to read bite size bits each day taking in suggestions and practising them.

At last even though I was still feeling very ill my beliefs were changing about myself and I had

HOPE; oh my hope, my new belief that I could change my life saved me for sure.

I learnt more about my personality traits. Having very high expectations of myself made me a perfectionist about how much I should achieve, how hard I should work and I carried on until the point of collapse and asked myself:

'Why did I feel the need to control everything?'

I found it hard to let go and let others do things, feeling I could do it all quicker and better while driving myself into the ground - this understanding was very enlightening!

This process raised more and more questions for me and I realised that I did not want to continue doing this. So, I reflected on my personality; explored how I was and what beliefs I had like:

'I have to work really hard to deserve a rest, I am not deserving of good things and I have to control everything'.

Writing this down feels shocking! When I thought about how hard I drove myself, I started to understand why I became ill. I invited all this stress into my life and then added more in by being so hard on myself. Writing all these things down was cathartic and allowed me to reflect on moments of clarity and any breakthroughs I had.

I realised how much I had pushed down inside myself. No one else had put this stuff inside me. It was no wonder I was ill with all this stuff rotting inside me, festering and dragging my health down. I imagined it as a festering compost heap literally!

It made sense to me that my body and mind were full of my unexpressed emotions and I had shut down and was literally overflowing with negative stuff; no wonder my mind and body shut up shop!

So I started to release a lot of unexpressed emotions making me very emotional but clearing and cleansing my mind was liberating. It felt like spring cleaning and dusting off the cobwebs.

I only saw Kim for 6 sessions (amazing) and it started me on my transformational journey. I wondered how I ended up where I was and then I considered how to move forwards successfully, healthily and positively. The journey of my transformation was beginning thank goodness!

Facing my unhappy marriage was a massive move forward for me and I realised how much stress I felt about it. I started to look at my marriage differently. I considered what I wanted, not what I could do to make things better! What were my beliefs about my marriage? What did I deserve in a marriage? Why had I lost myself in it and given him my power? Lots of questions but life changing questions!

I knew that asking these questions would lead me to the answers. As I got increasingly better, I looked differently at my marriage and realised we couldn't move forward if he refused to communicate with me or change. I was however too scared to leave the security of my marriage, to leave my beautiful home. I was also on long term sick leave so everything felt very insecure outside of this bubble so I allowed it to continue as it was. I was changing but he and our marriage were not.

Physically I started to stretch 5 minutes a day with yoga. I would increase this as I got stronger. Also, I made sure I sat outside each day. It was lovely to get fresh air and a fresh perspective. The more I did this, the better it felt and I could feel myself changing.

The difference my new found positive attitude made was fantastic. My new hopes and beliefs allowed me to make positive changes. The more I changed, the more I believed I could really change my whole life.

I had previously done a mindfulness course and I found that meditation was amazing but I did struggle to turn my focus inside myself and to just sit with the awful physical symptoms. My negative thoughts spun around my head causing an enormous challenge for me but I found it very powerful to just 'be' with whatever was going on inside me, to sit in that moment and accept whatever I felt.

I had spent years trying to get away from the debilitating pain and now I was deliberately focusing in on it. At first my conscious mind made up brilliant excuses why I should not meditate and practice mindfulness!

That power struggle with my mind was very enlightening but I got into the routine of just doing it twice a day at least; I had nothing but time and so I focused on sending myself love and healing instead of thinking 'poor me' and 'why am I in so much pain'? This was fantastic.

By then, I knew that I could not return to my social work career even if I wanted to as I was about to be medically retired; it was too stressful for me. I had learnt by then that this kind of stressful frontline work did not suit my personality, it did not suit who I was at all.

This was a struggle but I knew deep down that this was not my future. I wondered what other posts I could now do part time that would be more appropriate for me. It felt like part of me was stuck doing the same things over and over and over again and of course getting the same results!

I now use this saying:

'If you keep doing what you're doing, you will keep getting what you're getting!'

On my journey, I realised that I had to forgive some people to be able to move forward. It did not mean that what they did was OK but it meant that I stopped letting these things keep me in the past and drag myself down with unexpressed emotions and negativity.

I realised that at the end of the day I was the only person hurting by not forgiving them. By forgiving others using hypnotherapy and visualisation techniques, it made the forgiveness very powerful and afterwards I felt so free and liberated that I had done it and wished that I had done it a long time ago.

The other important thing for me to do was to forgive myself; this was massive for me. I wanted to forgive myself for what I had put myself, my body, my mind through; that was so very powerful. I was very gentle and loving in my forgiveness technique and I thanked myself for the learning that these awful 11 years had given me.

Now that is hard, to acknowledge that I had perpetuated the M.E and unhappiness myself through my choices, my actions and my beliefs. It had taken all those years to believe I had burnt myself out - no one else had. Even though my husband did not want me to leave my social work job because of the regular pay and pension I did not have to listen to him. I could have told him the job was too stressful, it was making my illness worse and I needed to leave. Sadly I had given my personal power to him so I just went along with it.

This is the power of recognising when we need to BE RESPONSIBLE for ourselves and our lives: powerful stuff! So again my subconscious beliefs, personality traits and past patterns were at play here.

Chapter 3: My lightbulb moment!

I had Hypnotherapy and it was very powerful. It made a massive impact on the changes I was making. Wondering why all the therapies I'd been using for years and all the programs I had used were not working, it became clear that the therapists I had been working with, were either focusing only on the body or the conscious mind. I made the powerful discovery that I needed to work with my subconscious, conscious mind and my body as they are of course connected!

I discovered the power of the subconscious mind and this opened up a whole lot of possibilities for me on my journey, for all my future clients and now for you on your journey. Neuroscientists are making discoveries that the subconscious makes up 95 to 98% of the mind: wow mind blowing! It was like the mismatched puzzle of my life that had been stuck for 11 years was starting to make sense and I was making a new healthy puzzle. This formed a happy positive picture!

I started to feel a bit better physically and my new found hope was growing. My confidence was increasing and I was feeling stronger in myself. I continued working on what I had learnt from and I was reading a lot about the Law of Attraction.

I was following the rules to manifesting and I wondered why it was not working, this took a while to work out but it hit me that I did not subconsciously believe that it would work. I did not believe that I deserved all these abundant things that I was asking for. Again, this went back to my subconscious beliefs. So I started wondering how I could change this with regard to the Law of Attraction.

By now another year had gone by. I had been waiting to be well enough to leave my husband, feeling frightened to do it - well petrified actually.

Even though I was so unhappy and it was contributing to my stress levels and illness, staying with him was safe and known.

Then another realisation hit me and lots of light bulbs were going off in my head! I realised that I had been waiting to get better so that I could then leave my husband but actually I needed to leave my husband to get better!

So, I prayed again in the early hours of the morning in the spare room on my hands and knees. This time I prayed for the strength to leave him. It was like standing at the top of a cliff looking down into the unknown and then being blindfolded so I could not see what was ahead of me. Wracked with fear, not knowing what would happen, as if my hands were tied behind my back I felt completely helpless and overwhelmed by an intense fear of the unknown.

I prayed to the universe, life, whatever is out there on the Wednesday, I was medically retired from my job on the Friday and I left our marital home on the Saturday!

I packed my car with my treasures, the most important treasure being my dog Bailey and I set off to start my new life in a new county with no job, no immediate money but with a new belief that all would be provided for abundantly.

I did it, leaping into the unknown and letting go. By trusting life, wonderful synchronicities and opportunities started to come my way, wow!

I loved hypnotherapy and the wellness coaching that I had experienced so I booked two courses in these subjects while I was still ill because my belief in myself and the Law of Attraction was getting stronger. My hope was so strong I went for it!

This was an extra special achievement as my husband was against me doing these courses. I again had listened to him initially but my new found belief in myself and the wonderful hope I felt was getting stronger hence I booked the courses. I had taken my power back and was starting to fly!

Once I had felt strong enough to leave my life with my ex-husband, I phoned the Hypnotherapy course company and asked where else they did their 10-month part - time course as I was moving counties; she said Norfolk or Devon. I had family or friends in either place so destiny was really helping me out there! So, I decided to move to Norfolk as my Dad offered me a home in his beautiful cottage with my beloved dog bless him. I'm eternally grateful to my Dad for this opportunity. My gorgeous Mum said I could move in with her and her husband but that would mean staying in the same area as my marital home and I knew I needed a whole new start.

It was really bizarre as I drove away from my marital home to feel an enormous weight lifting off my shoulders and over the coming months I started to gradually feel better just by having the stress of my job and my marriage taken away!

The night before I left I thanked my ex-husband for being the biggest teacher in my life as I'd learnt a huge amount about myself. What was the point of being bitter and blaming him; I'm proud of myself for being so loving, forgiving and positive.

I wished him all the happiness in the world and drove off into the sunset metaphorically speaking! I actually drove off into the rain, but no word of a lie once I was in Norfolk half of the sky was black and the other half was blue skies and there was the most beautiful rainbow and I drove under it to my sunnier destination. I know this sounds farfetched but it is absolutely true!

So, I started my new life with my beautiful dog and I absolutely loved it!

I set myself free, I did it!

At last I could do what I wanted: I could express myself freely, I could talk a lot, waffle if I wanted (as he hated that). I had healing time in the countryside and gradually started to put my head up and think about what I wanted to do.

I completed and passed both courses over that first year and absolutely love what I do now; it is such a privilege to support others and tell my transformational story. I feel so proud of myself for what I did, how I did it and now that I can share it with you. It truly is a dream come true (I'm getting emotional now).

As I reflect back on how I changed my life I can see how different I am now from that fearful, quiet peace maker. Then I felt my life was out of control, like a victim of life - powerless from not expressing my emotions.

Now I feel in control but letting go at the same time. I trust life, the universe and I feel so comfortable in my personal power that I'm free being who I truly am!

You have to let go and step or leap as I did into the unknown and then you are where you are meant to be; in the flow of your life. I realise that I kept swimming into the waves and tide instead of letting it take me and trusting that process. Now I trust and let go and boy it feels good!

Chapter 4: Going against my nature and personality

It is very interesting to write this and reflect on who I was then and how I wanted my life to be.

I realised that by acting and pretending I was better than I was, I had built a persona: I was wearing a mask. I showed this to people and then spent a lot of time becoming more and more introverted as I was not getting my own needs met. I was meeting everyone else's needs instead of my own – limiting beliefs dictated that.

Through my transformational process I learnt that by working as a front line social worker, I was actually for all those years going against my own true authentic self! By that I mean my personality, the nature of who I am and how I tick. I realised that I had the conflicting traits of being 'A Highly Sensitive Person' (I will describe in a moment) and an 'A' type personality.

There are personality type tests online and the results are interesting!

I discovered that I am an *'A type personality'* and for me that meant that I was:

-impatient

-a high achiever

-highly strung

-good at multi - tasking

-pushing myself very hard

-finding it difficult to accept failure (I felt I was a failure instead of thinking what I did had failed)

-competitive

-rushing around all the time

-frustrated easily

Yep, that fitted how I was and it's horrible to read them back now!

I then decided I wanted to be a *'type B personality'*; laid back and calm! I set my intention and have worked towards this and I am very aware of how I am now which keeps me in check!

Kim suggested I read the book 'The highly sensitive person' by Dr Elaine Aron, an American Psychologist. It was so enlightening! You can do a self-test online or from her book.

My ex-husband used to criticise me for being sensitive and it used to upset me a lot. Once I had understood what it meant I celebrated the fact as my sensitivity helps me all the time with my work. Clients often say I've hit the nail on the head with how they feel or I've taken them down a route of therapy at just the right time.

So now I shout to the world;

'I AM SENSITIVE AND I LOVE IT'!!

Chapter 5: From M.E to ME!

I have previously described what M.E is, and now I think of M.E as standing for;

Myself Expressed!

I had spent years of not expressing myself, pushing down all my emotions and pretending I was ok when I wasn't. I had learnt to do this as a child and it was a natural way of being.

Now

I view all of this as massive life lessons. These lessons dramatically changed my life and I am so thankful for these lessons; horrendous as they were at the time. It felt like it was all meant to be as I am now absolutely loving my life and work; supporting others who have given away their power, who are lost or are 'stuck' or who are blocked by their beliefs and thought patterns.

It's incredible to support and witness people change their lives to be who they truly are meant to be.

Chapter 6: Fear no longer drives my life

At the time, I did not know how much I had allowed fear to rule my life. I had given my mind, body and soul away to fear and I allowed it to totally consume me. I gave it full permission to march completely into my life and take over like a sergeant major calling all the shots. Blindly I listened and followed the demands and let it suck the life out of me!

I now wonder how I let it do this. How did I invite fear in and then hand my life over to it? I believe that when I gave my personal power away I let fear creep in and I got used to it being there. Then it had a party and said 'Woo Hoo! Let's take over', getting stronger and stronger with my full permission it stayed. Each time I got caught up, giving it my attention and focus, I gave in more and more to the fear.

I asked myself:

'Why did I allow fear to dominate my life?'

'What belief did I have about life?'

My self-limiting beliefs of 'I'm not good enough' and 'I'm not deserving of happiness and success', 'life is a fearful place' etc were very strong. I didn't know they were there for many years as I just went through life drifting on harbouring them and giving them life.

So, it was really important for me to acknowledge that I allowed this to happen and to recognise fear for what it is; a false thing that I made real by giving it my power and attention. I took full responsibility for letting fear take over and I realised that I had allowed fear to drive my life and I wanted to say good bye to it forever!

In Elizabeth Gilbert's book 'Big Magic', she talks about fear and creativity going on a road trip with her; I love this as she talks about giving fear a seat and a voice but saying to fear that it cannot make any decisions, cannot choose the music or the route and under no circumstance can fear drive!

This says it all. Think about this for your own life. Do you allow fear to drive your life? No longer do I allow that, I allow love and positivity to drive my life with travelling companions of compassion, unity, hope, success, health and forgiveness all by my side.

What do you choose to travel alongside you?

What do you allow to drive your life?

The choice is yours!

Chapter 7: Why other methods haven't worked

I worked with many clients when I was a social worker seeing how many people struggled to make changes in the long term, repeating the same cycles of behaviour and I became very interested in why this was.

Also, I had personally tried many other methods to change my life when I was ill with M.E and for years they did not work or did in the short term but didn't make permanent positive shifts. As I mentioned earlier, I discovered why they did not work; these methods and techniques were only working with the *conscious mind.*

I realised that I would need to also work with the subconscious mind and the body to make long lasting powerful positive changes.

Our present beliefs and thought patterns are a product of past programming into our subconscious minds when we were children: from our parents, carers, teachers and wider family members, society etc. As adults, we live from our beliefs in our subconscious mind. If they're self-limiting and negative about ourselves, these beliefs can hold us back from living the life we want and deserve.

Chapter 8: Transform your self-limiting beliefs

So, what negative beliefs or fears are holding you back?

Write them down.

Sometimes we know what our self-limiting beliefs are straight away from our conscious mind but sometimes we do not know because we have lived from them since childhood. You need to ask your subconscious mind what holds you back.

I changed these beliefs:

'I do not deserve to be successful or happy', I changed to 'I am very deserving of a very happy, successful and abundant life!'

'I am not good enough' I changed to 'I am more than good enough, I am fabulous!'

Plus, there were many more!

It is vital to make these changes on the subconscious level, otherwise you just keep going back to your default beliefs that are filed away in your subconscious mind.

I provide a hypnosis recording that guides you to change your self- limiting beliefs in my online programme (details at the end of my book).

Chapter 9: Blocks and challenges to changing your life

I came up with some great reasons why I should **not** have invested in the sessions with Kim, thank goodness I ignored them all! It is important to recognise them now so that you have an awareness of them when they come up.

These are the ones that I have noticed in other people as well as myself in the past:

- They are not willing to invest time, energy or money into transforming their life
- Resisting change
- Assuming their problems are unique (and they are not)
- Fearing the future (the unknown)
- Dwelling on their past mistakes
- Getting stuck in the past
- Not believing in themselves

- Believing that they are a failure rather than believing that something they did failed
- Giving up as it looks as if it will be too difficult
- Feeling too 'stuck'
- Still blaming other people or situations
- Not wanting to forgive others or themselves
- Their negative beliefs seem too strong
- Not feeling they deserve success
- Feeling they cannot visualise their abundant future
- Feeling things will get worse or that they will lose something
- Their unhappy life feels safe
- They have given away too much of their personal power

Do you resonate with any of these?

Take time to reflect on these and add any others that you recognise. ***Write them down.***

So now that you know what blocks and beliefs your mind throws up as obstacles to changing your life; what are you going to do?

Are you going to listen to all that negativity and continue as you are feeling stuck with whatever it is you struggle with?

Or are you going to for it, make the changes and live a fulfilled life?

The **fantastic news** is that all these can be overcome as you work through 'The Maya Method'. When you have an awareness of your self-limiting beliefs, you are half way there!

I was writing in my journal when I went through my journey of transformation and I started to record down what I was doing and how I was making these powerful life changes which is what I used to create the steps I use in 'The Maya Method'. I have used these steps with countless clients for great success and have adapted them to support you to transform your life. ***If I can do it, you can do it!***

Chapter 10: Your mind as your healer

Your mind is such an amazing tool, it is very powerful and under estimated! The first book I read that got me thinking when I was ill was 'How your mind can heal your body' by David R. Hamilton PhD. With his explanation about the power of positive thinking and believing, how thoughts change the make-up of the brain due to the chemicals produced in the process – I understood how powerful the mind really is.

I was also very aware of the power of placebos after being a social worker for years and reading research into medication trials. In these trials, one set of people were given the real drug and another set of people were given a placebo, a sugar pill. It was always wonderful to see that so many of the placebo group had positive results as they believed the pill would work!

Now you can see that what you already have is an amazing tool, an amazing healing tool: YOUR MIND!

Once you choose to BE RESPONSIBLE for your life and to change your mind and change your self-limiting beliefs, you too will understand the power of your mind.

I healed my mind and body with my own mind, my beliefs, my actions because instead of blaming others for my life; I CHOSE to BE RESPONSIBLE for me!

Chapter 11: Introducing the 6 steps of 'The Maya Method'

My method can support you to:

- Identify and change any self - limiting beliefs and self - sabotaging behaviour
- Move from living in fear to a place of love, positivity and abundance
- Thrive instead of drifting or surviving life
- Accept yourself
- Identify and reach your goals
- Boost your confidence and self-esteem
- Learn how to react to stress and difficult situations differently
- Deeply relax
- Manifest what you want in your life
- Create a positive daily routine

In my online programme, I guide you through the 6 steps and show you how to change your self-limiting beliefs so that you can change your life! It includes a powerful hypnosis recording for each of the 6 steps: more details at the end of the book.

The Powerful 6 steps of 'The Maya Method' are:

1) Taking Responsibility: awareness of the roles we take on

2) Forgiving and Releasing

3) Transform your self-limiting beliefs

4) Building your self-esteem and reconnecting to your personal power

5) How to thrive and manifest your desired life

6) Create your powerful positive daily routine

1) Taking responsibility: awareness of the roles we take on

This initial step is very important. If you don't take responsibility for your life, what will you do? Some people continue blaming others or think that life owes them something. This is a very negative place to live from and you will continue keeping yourself down or stuck in a place where you are not in control. You are powerless and at the mercy of whoever or whatever you blame. The cycle then continues.

You can do it: BE RESPONSIBLE for yourself...

It is about being responsible for your thoughts, actions and behaviours in the present moment - right here right now. I used to blame others for the way I was and it just took me deeper and deeper into the victim role that I had taken on, thinking 'poor me'.

Over the years in my career I noticed different roles that people took on, see if you can resonate with any of these:

- Victim
- Timid
- Bully
- Controller
- Judge

Of course, these roles can overlap and often play out subconsciously.

Victim

The victim can feel like life has been very unfair to them and sometimes that life owes them everything. They have given their power to this role, feeling like it is all out of their hands; that life happens to them without their input. They will have probably given their power to anyone that they have experienced negative or traumatic situations with.

Now of course those kind of situations are awful and can dramatically affect how you feel but we have the CHOICE to move forward differently, free from this powerless role - feeling 'poor me'.

I used to say: 'Oh they/ he /she makes me feel', that is a powerless expression and that is why I used it as I had given my power away. Now I realise that nobody can make me feel anything!

It is my choice how I react to people and situations; they can't MAKE me feel anything thankfully.

Timid

People who take on the Victim role can be timid or take on other roles as well, but the timid role is when people normally have very low self-esteem. They accept this as who they are having always been like that. They normally like to stay in their comfort zone and are 'yes people', feeling powerless too but quietly so.

They are also powerless and are fearful of most things and prefer to stick to their known, comfortable routine, even if that makes them very unhappy or sick. The safe feeling keeps them there and their situation matches their self-limiting beliefs.

Bully

The bully normally has self-limiting beliefs about not feeling worthy or they have low self-esteem but they cope with this by being loud and aggressive to others so they are bullying others whilst protecting themselves - before they are found out. They normally surround themselves in a gang to protect them further but they want to be in the lead role.

Controller

This person often feels compelled to control everything as they feel out of control of their life or aspects of their life, this normally starts in childhood.

This control may be over their environment which can lead to an obsessive-compulsive disorder or into controlling other people acting as a bully or as an eating disorder, compulsive eater etc. Something becomes comforting for them, it feels good, even if it is unhealthy or negative.

Judge

Someone who judges or criticises others normally feels that way about themselves or fears that it will happen to them. It is a projection of their own feelings onto others: I used to be like that! I would judge and criticise others inwardly for not working flat out all day like I was feeling that they should too!

As I did not feel worthy of resting or taking it easy, I would push myself very hard and expect others to too. I was projecting my negative and ridiculous expectations onto them. Gosh I did that for years!

I found it so hard to let other people just be themselves: it used to drive me mad! To be healthy in our selves we will accept all the beautiful variety of people and personalities that exist.

The common denominator with all these roles is normally very low self-esteem; in simple terms, self-esteem is how much we like or dislike ourselves and how worthy and deserving we feel of good things happening to us - these are the big clues.

Any of these roles are normally accompanied with a deep sense of unhappiness and can end up spiralling into anxiety or spiralling down into depression.

So by letting go of your role you will be the true, real you - the person you have always meant to be!

The Vase!

I think of the psychological self within the body as a Vase! I believe that over the years we fill our vase up with unexpressed emotions, guilt, shame, anger, not forgiving others or ourselves, jealousy, loss and grief etc. So, our vase gets full up. The bottom starts to fester like a compost heap and it gives off unhealthy gases that make us sick and weighs us down so much and when the vase is full it starts to overflow, spilling over into our lives as a mental health or physical health issue.

When it does this, it can lead to out of control anger, disease (which I believe is the body in dis– ease with itself), anxiety, depression, heart attack etc. Our vase is too full of our past negative emotions it needs emptying! You may need to forgive others. This does not mean you are saying what they did was OK but you are freeing yourself from carrying around that huge negative weight of not forgiving them.

My vase is now empty and I have energising water in it with beautiful quartz crystals in the bottom and the most stunning colourful vibrant flowers that are fresh and never wilt!

I also see our emotional selves as having a hole that we fill with all sorts of things to try and feel whole and comforted! I used to fill my hole with drinking, casual sex and wild partying in my 20's, then with working very hard in my career as a social worker in my 30's, feeling very stressed out and eating way too much sugar leading to the M.E in my 40's; all due to my past actions and beliefs and my vase spilled over! So, life began for me moving into my 50's: Woo Hoo! I no longer feel the need to fill myself with anything as I naturally feel content and whole, leaving wonderful space for love and positivity!

The hypnosis recording I use for this step on my online programme guides you to take responsibility for you and to change the role you have lived by so far.

2) Forgiveness and Releasing unexpressed emotions

When you choose not to forgive someone it does not affect them but it affects you as you keep that negative energy inside you.

Forgiveness isn't about saying to them that what they did is right but it is letting go of negative energy that would otherwise fester inside you and make you ill physically, mentally or both.

If you learnt not to express your emotions like I did, it can make you ill especially if you are unconsciously holding onto blame, guilt, anger or shame. As children, we take on issues and blame ourselves for things that were not our responsibility at all. They eat you up and fester inside you affecting your adult life until you change it.

Forgiveness is what takes us on the journey towards healing ourselves and moving forward positively. When you forgive, you take back your power so you can control your fate and your feelings. Forgiveness is for you so that you can free yourself. This is part of taking responsibility for yourself.

By forgiving you move from being a victim to being a warrior, determining your own strength and fate.

You may need to forgive yourself for doing or not doing something; otherwise this can eat you up on the inside and pull you down.

I use a very powerful technique in the hypnosis recording I provide in my online programme to help you move forward through letting go and forgiving.

3) Transform your self-limiting beliefs

The roles we take on are driven by the beliefs we have about ourselves and the world around us. As I have discussed already, these beliefs are a result of past programming into your subconscious mind from childhood. We pick up these beliefs from our parents, families, care givers, teachers, friends, television and from society in general.

When you have these patterns of beliefs they attract situations and people to you that fit that negative belief so it becomes a self-fulfilling prophecy. I hear people say, 'I told you so, I knew that would happen!' The negative thing that they expected happened and it fits their pattern and belief.

This feels strangely comfortable because it is such a good fit. Does it feel good though: positive, supportive, abundant, amazing? I doubt it very much, they normally hold us back and drive our life from a place of fear.

When you have taken responsibility for your life and you start to have a deeper awareness of your self-limiting beliefs you can reflect and notice your thoughts and negative expressions. The most common ones being:

'I'm not good enough' or 'I'm unlovable'.

The first belief was one of mine as you know and now I truly believe that 'I am more than good enough: I am fabulous!'

You may have heard of The Law of Attraction. I go into this more on my online programme. It is basic quantum physics: what you believe and put out, you attract back to you on an energetic level. It works with your beliefs, your thoughts, expectations and actions so if they are negative, guess what; they manifest as negative. Then the cycle continues.

This is what happened to me, I was practising it but my self-limiting beliefs were attracting what I believed which was more of the same negative things I had been through.

It is very important that you change your self-limiting beliefs to new positive beliefs supporting what you want in life, but you may not know or be aware of what your self-limiting beliefs are. This is why working with your subconscious mind to identify and change your beliefs is so important and powerful.

A situation occurs or we learn something when we are children, a new belief is then formed from our reaction, then this belief is filed away in our subconscious mind and we live from this belief.

When other situations occur in our life our conscious mind looks into our subconscious mind and looks to find a match and if your belief is negative, it ignores it even if it is a positive thing happening like someone giving you a huge compliment as your conscious mind says no it does not match your subconscious belief. So you end up rejecting that positive gift or worse, rejecting a big positive opportunity.

Then that negative belief gets stronger; the pattern gets deeper and dictates your negative thoughts and behaviour. Sometimes this leads to depression where your thoughts spiral down or into anxiety where your thoughts spiral up out of control. Anxiety is your subconscious mind protecting you from harm but it gets confused about what is harmful to you and ends up keeping you in an anxious state about everything.

We then attract situations and other people who match our beliefs, and it goes on and on for the whole of our life time unless we change our beliefs at our subconscious level.

I have heard so many clients over the years say: 'oh this is just how I am' and they go on accepting it - being powerless. They have gone through life looking through glasses tainted with pain or negative beliefs and just accept them. You do not have to accept them anymore!

It's your choice ultimately;

'Keep doing what you are doing and you will keep getting what you are getting from life'! This keeps you 'stuck'...........

I changed my beliefs and my life; so I believe anyone can!

So, to support you in changing your self-limiting beliefs and to let go of all that stuff you have subconsciously held onto that is dragging you down, I provide a hypnosis recording using Inner Child therapy techniques which are part of my online programme for this step.

4) <u>Building your self-esteem and reconnecting to your personal power</u>

With new positive beliefs, well and truly programmed into your subconscious mind, it is like looking at life differently through positive coloured glasses to suit your taste!

So, next you build up your self-esteem with the help of your new positive beliefs as the new foundations of your strong house.

You can tell I am a visual person I have used a vase, a hole and now a house to describe my techniques!

Self-esteem is not to be mixed up with confidence. Your confidence levels fluctuate depending on what you are doing. Someone can be very confident at work but very low in confidence socially for example. Self-esteem fluctuates as well as confidence depending on how you feel about yourself but generally self-esteem is how worthy you feel, how much you like yourself, how much you love yourself ultimately.

So score your self- esteem levels generally as a percentage; this will be good to do again after you have made the changes to your life.

The hypnosis recording for this step is reconnecting you to your personal power.

5) How to thrive and manifest your desired life

Now you have changed your self-limiting beliefs to positive supportive beliefs the world is your oyster as they say!

Within this you will accept yourself and believe in yourself, identify your goals and dream big!

As I previously stated I use The Law of Attraction which started to work for me once I had changed my self -limiting beliefs and I was living from my new beliefs of:

'I can do it'

'I am more than good enough, I am fabulous!'

'I believe in myself'

'I am very successful'

'I deserve and receive an abundance of everything life has to offer'!

(Wow I love this process so much!)

Changing your self-limiting beliefs is the KEY!!

Due to the fact that I used to live from a place of fear and negativity, I was ATTRACTING what I put out.

Now that I choose to live from a place of Love and Positivity, my life is dramatically different; fantastic, incredible!

So, once you have changed your beliefs at the subconscious level using my programme you can start manifesting!

Do remember though, you cannot manipulate or control other people's lives with The Law of Attraction!

The Law of Attraction steps are:

*State what you want - Be specific about the elements that you want but keep it open so that it does not limit you (i.e. where exactly your dream house will be to keep your options open). Write it down, cut pictures out and stick them onto a vision board and look at them every day (put the board somewhere you pass regularly).

*Believe and perceive it - Visualise that it is already in your life and plan your life around it. Watch your language though i.e. saying it 'will' means it will be in the future and it stays in the future! Make sure it is in the present tense of already having it. A good way of doing that is saying or writing down on a Gratitude list; thank you so much for the wonderful …….. that is in my life, I love that it is……. supporting me…I am so happy and content with ….. (Fill in the blanks!)

*Use the Law of Action - Move towards what you want, look at houses, plan your interior, go to shops, look at travel brochures and plan when you are going, write it on the calendar! Apply for jobs, take the opportunities:

STEP OUT OF YOUR COMFORT ZONE!

Say YES to life!

If you keep saying no to life, you miss out!

*Be ready for it! Keep your radar up for synchronicities, opportunities, things that resonate with you as these things may not make sense to you or seem like you will benefit from it but there may be wonderful opportunities waiting for you. Go and talk to people you are drawn to, they might not help you but they then introduce you to someone who does or that gives you the opportunity to help others as it is all about giving and receiving with the ENERGY of the UNIVERSE.

<u>For example:</u>

I was invited to go to a networking meeting; I was not that keen and did not think as a Hypnotherapist I would meet that many clients there. I got home and then reflected on it as I had a feeling that this was going to be very positive for some reason.

So I went with that feeling and joined, I did not just get clients from these meetings but I had great fun, met loads of great people, enjoyed the socialising and made contacts and the most amazing things started to happen!

I was offered session swops for their amazing skills and it transformed my business branding, promotional material and visibility making my business more professional.

Here are the amazing swops I had:

-Marketing

-Website content

-Graphic design

-Professional photography

-Banner

-Videos for my website

(I have listed these wonderful people in my Acknowledgments section at the beginning of this book in case you want to contact them as I highly recommend them all!)

Just as all these were put into place, I was invited to become a teacher on the amazing online 'Transformation TV' of Hidden Teachers around the world and here I am writing a book! I was professionally ready for this invite and I had manifested it through the Law of Attraction.

Wow, so good to reflect on how I got here and I am so proud of myself and grateful to all those who helped me get here.

So, if I had not listened to that feeling and joined the Networking group I would not be in this amazing place now!

In my online programme, I support you to reflect on where you are now: where you want to be and how to use the Law of Attraction to get you there using the hypnosis recording for this step.

Abundance is waiting for you, it's not an exclusive club!

6) Create your powerful positive daily routine

What really helped me when I was sick was to create a routine, so however ill, negative or down I felt it kept me going as I was clearing my blocks and self-limiting beliefs.

My routine still is:

*Grounding myself

I lie in bed and imagine roots coming out of my feet down into the core of the earth and I wrap them around 1 or 2 powerful beautiful crystals and pull the energy up through my roots and through my whole mind and body: it feels really good!

*Giving thanks and sending love and healing out

When I wake up (I naturally wake up calmly before my alarm goes off as I have trained my subconscious mind!) I lie in bed saying to myself all that I am grateful for: my body that works, my home, food, security, loved ones, including our beautiful planet.

*Writing in my journal

I write down my thoughts which is a great way to express my feelings and I change any negative thoughts to positive thoughts or goals to make positive changes.

*Gratitude list

It is great to start the list off with the big things in life and then you can add the daily positive things that happen, all the small things like someone doing a positive thing for you or giving you a compliment. Another great way of doing this is to write positive things down, pop them in a jar or bowl and look through them when you want a boost or to see how well you have done.

*Stretching your body, walking, exercise or yoga

I get up earlier and have time to calmly enjoy doing this. I don't watch television so this allows me to go to bed at 10/10.30pm and get up feeling refreshed and alive at 6am even in the depths of winter which I did not want to do before! Even if you just do 15 minutes of something!

I also do a yoga class once a week and a Pilates class once a week; however busy or exhausted I am, these are set in stone in my diary and I am committed to myself to go and of course I love the sessions once there!

Being outside in nature is so important for me. I crave it if I don't get out into nature every day. Pulling up energy into my solar plexus chakra (under our ribs) using colour whilst breathing in the lovely country air. It energises me and grounds me and I include my Mindfulness practice out there.

*Mindfulness

Taking time throughout our busy day to just stop and notice the beauty around us is great. Even if I am in a city surrounded by concrete or it is a dark rainy day I will always find something positive or beautiful to admire.

* Putting nourishing foods and drinks into our bodies that energise us rather than drain us

If it is naturally grown and not processed it is nourishing! If it is highly processed and packaged it is not! I eat a rainbow of colours of foods which look great and are great being organic where possible! I avoid wheat, dairy and sugar too as these drain me and are inflammatory to the body.

*Do what you feel passionate about!

So many people spend hours and hours doing a job they don't like or worse that they hate. (I highly recommend that you contact Hilary Lees from Essence Coaching for career / work transition support, she is a very experienced and amazing coach).

What do you love to do? Reflect on this and write it down.

Incorporate these things into your life and love the way you feel! Start to research about what your dream job is, do a course in your spare time, do a little voluntary work (I did and it worked brilliantly on my C.V when I wanted to be a social worker).

*React to stress differently

Say stop to yourself before you go off on your usual way to deal with stress, this then gives you space to take deep breaths to calm yourself down. Say positive affirmations to yourself;

'I can deal with any situation'

'I am calm and confident'

In my online programme, I have included a deeply relaxing hypnosis recording for you to change how you react to stress, to believe in yourself and that change is effortless.

*Expecting great things to happen every day!

I hear a lot of people saying 'What if I am late and what if I cannot do this? Of course, it then attracts the things you do not want!'

So I say:

'What if I have an amazing day?!'

'What if the most fantastic thing happens to me today?'

Say these out loud and notice the difference in how you feel saying these. The positive statements will energise you and you feel so much better!

*Having 'Me time!'

This is normally the practice that gets pushed out and filled with everyday tasks or work. It may just be to read your favourite magazine, have a quiet bath without being disturbed or doing an exercise class but it is so important to feel you have some time for just you.

Some people will watch television for hours a week and not really watch anything that is interesting or enjoyable to them anyway. Is this you sometimes?

Switch the television off and do something you love!

*Meditation

By just closing your eyes for a few minutes and taking deep breaths, bringing yourself into the present moment and focusing on your breath. Continually bringing your mind back to this keeps you in the moment. Doing this just before bedtime is brilliant to put you in the right mind set and you have a deeper more refreshing sleep.

*Listening or reading positive things before bed

A lot of people watch the negative News before bed: it is not good! The best thing I do is to listen to one of my hypnosis recordings (it was weird at first listening to my own voice but great now!) and I drift off straight away and have a lovely deep refreshing sleep and my subconscious mind is learning something new, positive and it re-programs my subconscious, the hard drive of my computer!

What will your powerful positive daily routine consist of?

The hypnosis recording for this step in my online program is deeply relaxing and empowering.

Chapter 12: Your next step!

Imagine how wonderful you will feel making all the positive changes that you want:

Just take some time now to visualise what you want in your life; how will it look……

It feels wonderful, right?

I can support you to explore what is holding you back and to move forward positively to live a happy abundant life!

So now:

If you would like to do the deeper work to change your self - limiting beliefs with 'The Maya Method', you can do this via my online programme; please see my website (details below). The program includes 6 videos, 6 hypnosis recordings to listen to and a PDF.

I use coaching, counselling skills, inner child therapy and NLP (neuro linguistic programming) techniques and hypnotherapy with 'The Maya Method' to make these lasting powerful changes in your subconscious mind.

To find out more information, purchase my online programme or to book sessions please see:

www.mayawellbeing.co.uk or email karen@mayawellbeing.co.uk

References

Aron, E Ph.D. (1998) The Highly Sensitive Person. Three Rivers Press. New York .

Gilbert, E. (2015) Big Magic: Creative Living Beyond Fear. Bloomsbury Publishing.

Dr. Hamilton, D. (2008) How your mind can heal your body. Hay House. London.

www.thegracecharityforme.org/what.asp (accessed 30/06/16).

About the Author

Karen has a Diploma in Hypnotherapy and Counselling skills and a Parks Inner Child Therapy for Trauma and Abuse specialist skills Diploma and a Diploma in Social Work.

She is also a Wellness Coach and is a Hypnobirthing and Fertility practitioner as well as a Reiki Healer.

Karen is a number 1 best-selling author and runs empowering workshops, personal development retreats and presents her powerful inspiring talks in varying venues. She is passionate about empowering you to live your true authentic abundant life that you want and deserve.

Her social work career consisted of supporting people experiencing severe and enduring mental health issues in psychiatric units and in the community. Then supporting people in a multi -

disciplinary stroke rehabilitation team on a recovery ward and out in the community.

Previously to that Karen was a chef and catering manager in London and Kent.

She lives in a lovely village in Norfolk, England with her beloved dog Bailey!

Printed in Great Britain
by Amazon

42393022R10059